Season's End

Season's End

Poems by

B. A. France

© 2021 B. A. France. All rights reserved.
This material may not be reproduced in any form, published,
reprinted, recorded, performed, broadcast,
rewritten or redistributed without
the explicit permission of B. A. France.
All such actions are strictly prohibited by law.

Cover design by Shay Culligan
Cover Image: "Sakura Cherry," Library of Congress, Prints &
Photographs Division, LC-DIG-jpd-01197

ISBN: 978-1-954353-11-4

Kelsay Books
502 South 1040 East, A-119
American Fork, Utah, 84003

For
Kat and Josephine,
and their garden friends

Acknowledgments

The author thanks the editors of the following journals where versions of these poems first appeared:

Akitsu Quarterly

cattails

Chrysanthemum

OPEN: Journal of Arts & Letters

Contents

Preface

swallowtail in flight	13
Tunnel Vision	14
Foxtrot	16
red gladiolus	18
lone monarch	19
White Wings	20
Hybridization	22
hydrangea blossoms	24
a petal spirals	25
In Flight	26
Dogwood	28
snare drum of rain	30

About the Author

Preface

a flock of haibun
observing summer's end
...scattered poems

Whitehall Bay
2020

swallowtail in flight

working over the phlox blooms

thoughtless work

Takuan wrote forget the mind

so you can do all things

Tunnel Vision

Standing in the looping country road, looking away from the creeks that lead toward the bay and the promise of open waters, away from the possibility of the wider world, the view is like a tunnel, narrowing. Oaks, elms, tulip trees stretch overhead, branches reaching across the open space where, if it were midday, they would be soaking up the sun as the leaves turned their flat bodies toward the glow and heat. But it is not midday. It is dusk, past dusk really, twilight, and those flat bodies instead shade out the luminosity of a half-moon. They are a dark tunnel stretching out in front of me, seemingly tightening until they unfurl at the edge of the pasture. The expanse of grazing room stretching further away from the creeks and offering the thistle and stiffened grass to the sheep who are not outdoors. No smell of them to accompany the loud moment of twilight. Not quiet, not still, instead alive and loud with the muted jostle of those flat bodies in a brief breath of wind. The joyful noise of the frogs, moist with an afternoon thunderstorm. Crickets reaching crescendo, exulting in their contribution to the chorus. As I breathe deeply, the leaf mold, the debris, the wet richness, hangs under the sheer breeze. In the luster at the end of the darkened tunnel, the split rails offer parallel dark lines of shadow from post to post, wrapping outward as the looping road curves out of sight. The unquiet quiet of the night at the edge of the wood, the stretching fence line, the curving road.

                    empty roads
                    offer another path
                    ...warming wind

Foxtrot

Suddenly she is there. One moment the paved blackness was empty, then the shrewd fox is in the middle of it, looking back at me. A momentary tip of the head. Acknowledgment. Her low body and red hair sleek along the ground as she stares for the briefest moment to see if I'm moving. But I'm not. I'm frozen still as if I was that young cottontail in the grass, thinking a lack of movement is safety. Her ears stand at attention. I expect her to be gone as instantly as she appeared, slipping through the weeds and tiger lilies on the side of the looping wooded lane, disappearing into the thicket of undergrowth and fallen limbs from the recent thunderstorms, back toward the creek in search of a meal. But she isn't. Instead, she pivoted with such grace that her direction confused me, and then she was headed away, in the middle of the lane. She sauntered breezily, showing the world that her trot is anything but a dance, as if the long blacktop which curved out of sight was there not for human transportation and the noisey, malodorous pickup trucks, but instead conveniently added to simplify her evening patrol. Then, effortlessly, she shot me another glance. I was still motionless and her look alone spoke, reminding me that she is the main character in the drama of this wood and I am still but a bit player, maybe just an extra.

She trots on.

                              mourning dove
                              calls in the warm silence
                              hovering clouds

red gladiolus

reaching tall and top heavy

toward the sky

falling over we cut stems

in the vase a second life

lone monarch

working over the blossom

focused diligence

and loneliness gives way to

the freedom of solitude

White Wings

He jounces and jostles above the gravel lane and I slow my pace to watch him ahead of me. Busy white wings, dollar-sized, in constant motion. Not as big as silver dollars, instead those new ones, with Jean Baptiste hoisted on Sacagawea's back and her knowing, world-wise gaze over her shoulder, looking back at you as if thinking: I see what you're going to do to this place. The Cabbage White seems like such a humdrum, plodding name for something as beautiful as a butterfly. And he is anything but plodding as he moves several feet above the gray-white gravel. As if one of the stones had cut the bonds of the lane and slipped up into the air, transformed, to fly away. He wiggles and moves, as if flying through an unseen mechanical turbulence. Up and down, left and right, but ever moving forward, down the lane, toward his destination. None of the graceful glides of the black swallowtail that sometimes joins him flying in our wood, instead wings in constant motion. Alone, he looks like he is working so hard. It is not the dance that Mary Oliver saw, the seven brothers and sisters in an elaborate vertical waltz. But despite the up, the down, the left, the right, he continues forward, broken free, in constant progress forward.

> under the maple
> summer ivy claims space
> crawling over stones

Hybridization

The oaks are spread throughout, the ragged hollies unable but trying to climb to their majestic heights, the sleek tulips rushing upward among them. He shuffles back through the lawn, eyes up on the canopy overhead, fully leafed out in the late summer heat. His feet move slowly in trainers instead of the leather and steel toes he surely wore for decades. We thought we identified the tree as a pin oak, among the red oaks and white oaks of our wood. The *quercus*. "Nope," he says, "I think it hybridized. Sometimes they do that on their own." On their own. Best estimation, the white oak, evolved over centuries for this sometimes sodden, bayside ground, was not quite right for our back wood. It mixed with the pin oak and grew quietly for half a century before homes, eventually our shed, were built nearby. Hybridization. Evolved. Unnoticed for eight decades. Not cataclysm. Not havoc. Not revolution. Change, one being at a time. One soul at a time. How progress starts, not with digital speed, or with deliberated fanfare. With singular change. One being, hybridized. Leading to another. If it can survive. Hopefully. He continues to gaze upward at the canopy, "beautiful tree though."

>
> not disruption
> natures real progress
> an unknown tree

hydrangea blossoms

blue pink pom poms dancing

mid-summer breeze

the garden reminds me

glory comes cheering others

a petal spirals

onto the long blue flagstone

last summer heat

in still humid air autumn

doesn't seem quite like the end

In Flight

Fescue, dollar weed, and crabgrass beneath us we watch the landing pattern of our own private air show. Our white winged friend was there, like a tiny tourist flitting around seeing the sights. The Black Swallowtail, soaking up the last of the afternoon heat through her jet wings, freckled with the vibrance of blue and yellow spots. Such a beautiful long glide. Over top of the purple basil's flowering minarets, she descended alongside the sleek lavender leaves. Calming next to the fluttering exuberance of her white-winged companion. Her Eastern Tiger cousin studiously worked over the blooms of the Hot Lips. With speed but no sound, the Skimmer screamed through the waist high peaches of our craggy little tree. The dragonfly's slim white tail rushed past as he banked left and right through the graceful paths of the butterflies. The crickets behind us in the back wood sang on.

>taking to the air
>ignoring the audience
>a dance in the sun

Dogwood

It happens the same way as every summer ends. At least, it has since we first moved ourselves to this wood. Color comes to the leaves in the first place we see every morning. The dogwood directly out the front door begins to fade and the deepening colors present themselves to the world. It is the same tree that is the last to leaf out each spring. And we wonder if maybe the previous year had been her last. Should we replace her? Should we head for the nursery, or maybe the native plant sale with the naturalists to remind us of what belongs here? No, the dogwood surprises us. Though, after all these years, it should not be a surprise. She flowers and the delicate white blooms fill the air and the sightlines through the screen door. The leaves come. And we're reminded that the dogwood belongs here. Or, at least, belongs more than we do. She was here stretching her roots toward the oak and the azalea, getting a head start on us before we even thought of our own roots, our own connection to this place. She is the first to fade, the first color we notice out the front screen door. But maybe she just enjoys her rest. And why not?

> orange yellow red
> begin their siege of green
> omens in leaves

snare drum of rain

on limp leaves

not yet dropped

gray wet dreary weeks

until the beauty of snow

Season's End

About the Author

B. A. France is a poet and writer who lives and works in the Chesapeake Bay watershed and is lucky to live with a Master Gardener who shares a love of the natural world. His poetry has appeared in numerous journals, including *Modern Haiku, Cold Moon Journal, Last Leaves,* and others.

Made in the USA
Columbia, SC
09 August 2021